Wink, Blink, and Pink

Written by
Debbie Strayer

Illustrations by
Joy Majewski

New Sounds:

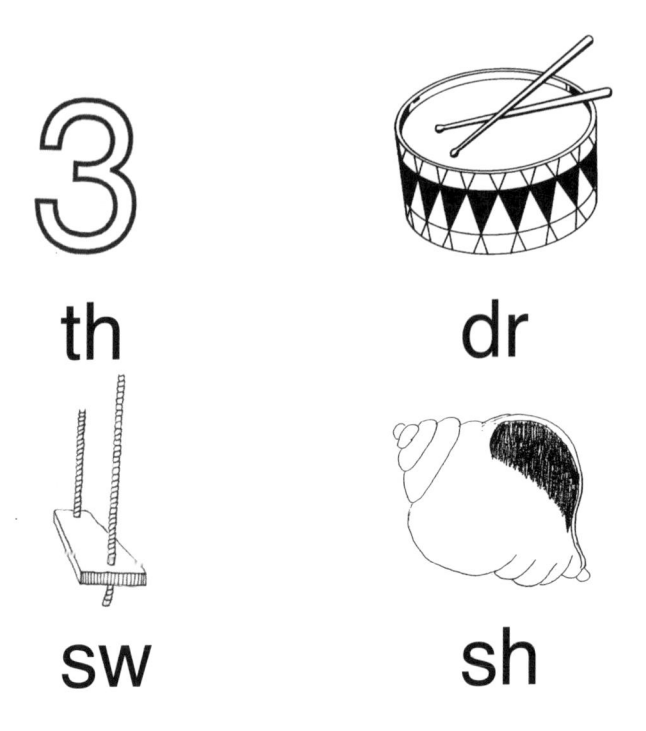

th

dr

sw

sh

(Note: The pictures indicate the sound, not the spelling.)

Common Sense Press

© 1998 by Common Sense Press

Printed 09/15

8786 Highway 21 • Melrose, FL 32666

ISBN 1-880892-59-6

Three shells are in the sand. They are Wink, Blink, and Pink.

1

They can stand on the land. It is grand!

The shells fell in the swell. To drink they must sink.

I think he can wink.
Just look in my hand.

Wink, Blink, and Pink are grand. I trust they are well.

Uh-oh! They fell!
Plink! Clink!

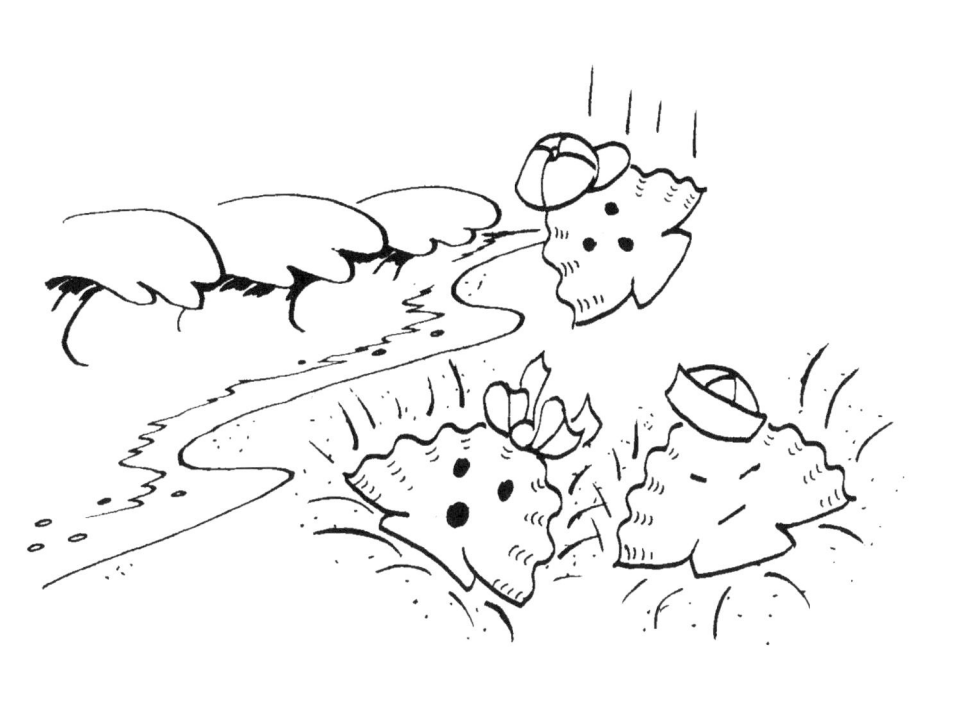

The shells have a crust. They fell in the dust and the sand.

All is well, they will tell you. The shells love the land and the sand.

New Words:

th	**dr**	**sh**	**sw**	**_ell**
think	drink	shells	swell	tell
			well	

New Sight Words:

three   uh-oh   look   my

Review Words:

are	in	can	all	on
they	it	and	will	to
the	is	I	he	you
love				

Word Families:

-ink	-and	-ust
plink	stand	must
drink	sand	just
sink	land	trust
think	grand	crust
wink	hand	dust
clink		
Blink		
Pink		